POEMS AND QUOTES VOL -2

SHREERAJ MENON

Contents

Contents

Contents

Contents

Contents

Preface

This book consists of some of the poems and Quotes written by the author on the theme of Love, Nature and general day to day aspects of life. There are some inspirational quotes too. Love includes Love found, Love lost and love re-awakened. Similarly, Nature consists of the importance of nature and how people mis-utilize the nature to their own advantages without going for the aftereffects. General consists of the general aspects of life which goes on with people and the surroundings.

Acknowledgements

I would like to thank my friends who inspired me in writing the Poems and Quotes which I used to say out and forget it. I would also like to thank Your Quote platforms and all its members and groups for allowing me and inspiring me to write my contents on its platform. I would also like to thank Notion Press and all its members who allowed me to publish my contents through their platform and the time-to-time guidance which they gave me to correct my errors.

1. Addiction

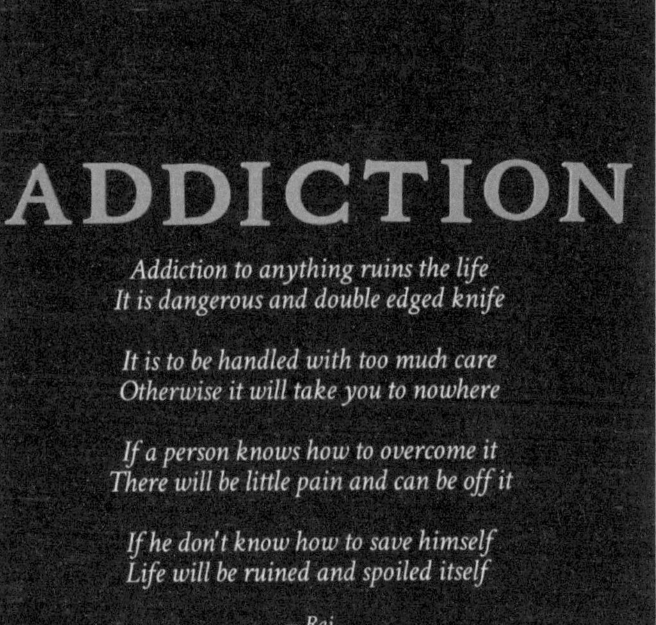
ADDICTION
Addiction to anything ruins the life
It is dangerous and double edged knife
It is to be handled with too much care
Otherwise it will take you to nowhere
If a person knows how to overcome it
There will be little pain and can be off it
If he don't know how to save himself
Life will be ruined and spoiled itself
– Raj

Enter Caption

2. After my death

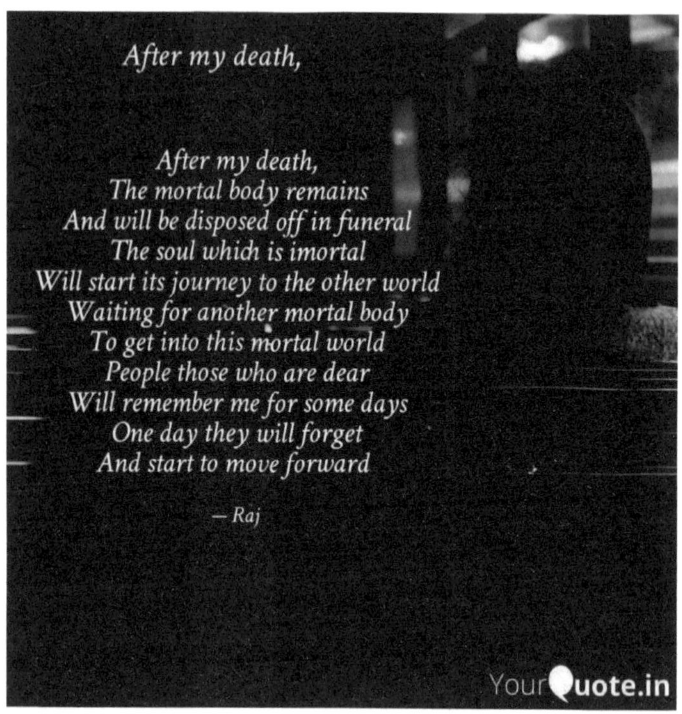
After my death,
After my death,
The mortal body remains
And will be disposed off in funeral
The soul which is imortal
Will start its journey to the other world
Waiting for another mortal body
To get into this mortal world
People those who are dear
Will remember me for some days
One day they will forget
And start to move forward
— Raj
YourQuote.in

Enter Caption

3. World of Darkness

Alone in the world of darkness
I wait eagerly for the light to return

Would love to have a life partner
But fate moved me to a corner

Hoping for a better day to come
People who knows will be some

Let the fate to play the game
Every time won't be the same

— Raj

YourQuote.in

Enter Caption

4. Art of being in love

The art of being in love was never taught by anybody
It is a natural process as the nature itself is based on love

Hatred is a human based phenomenon which prevails
As it is the end of the universe more and more hatred remains

Life line of the universe is based on pure and only pure love
Ninety percent of the people here are based on artificial love

Sustainability of the universe is at stake in this case
That is the very reason where injustice is very high and is at stake

— Raj

YourQuote.in

Enter Caption

5. What is Aura?

//Aura//

What is Aura?
Aura is the subtle body and is a mass of energy. It can be seen by anyone with a little effort. Clairvoyant skills are not necessary to see aura but interpretation of it is a bit difficult if you don't understand it. Some may see it in colours which represents the colour of your 7 chakras. Rainbow colour V. I. B. G. Y. O. R. While some may see it as a pure white light. The only thing which you have to observe is whether it posses a black patch. If you see black colour patches then it is the negative energy which is to be addressed with care and removed.

— Raj

YourQuote.in

Enter Caption

6. Beauty Means

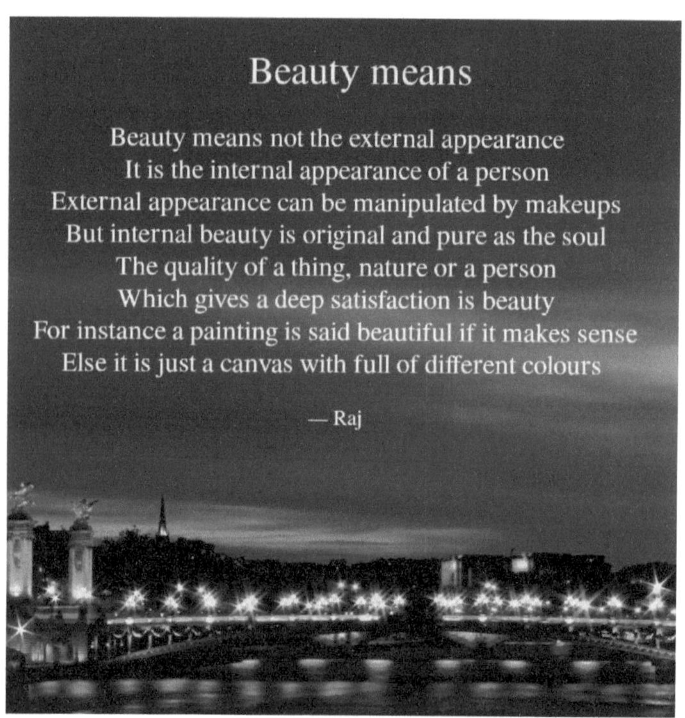
Beauty means
Beauty means not the external appearance
It is the internal appearance of a person
External appearance can be manipulated by makeups
But internal beauty is original and pure as the soul
The quality of a thing, nature or a person
Which gives a deep satisfaction is beauty
For instance a painting is said beautiful if it makes sense
Else it is just a canvas with full of different colours
— Raj

Enter Caption

7. To forget the past

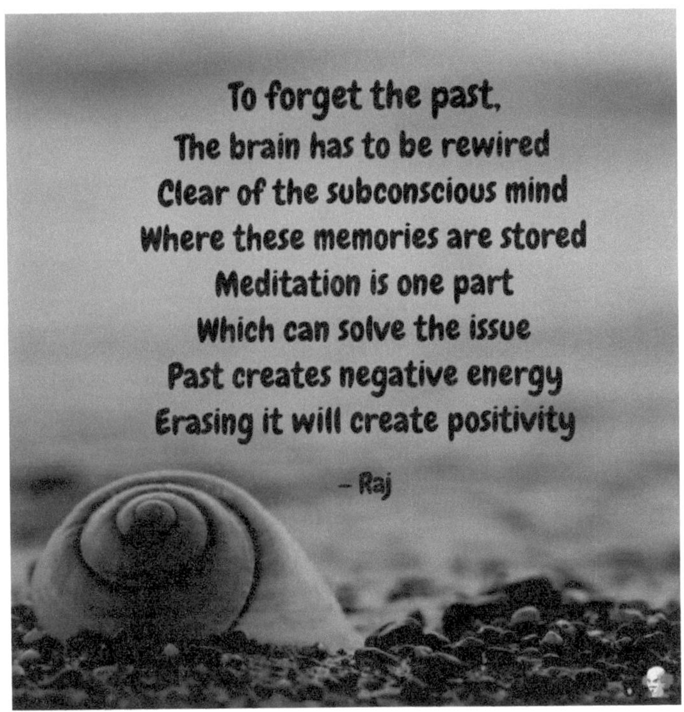

To forget the past,
The brain has to be rewired
Clear of the subconscious mind
Where these memories are stored
Meditation is one part
Which can solve the issue
Past creates negative energy
Erasing it will create positivity
- Raj

Enter Caption

8. Destiny

We can't change our destiny, but
We can change course of our destiny
Destiny is what it happens
The way it is destined
The path towards it can be changed
With hardwork and belief in yourself
No one else can change your destiny
So move forward and face your destiny
— Raj

Enter Caption

9. Two choices

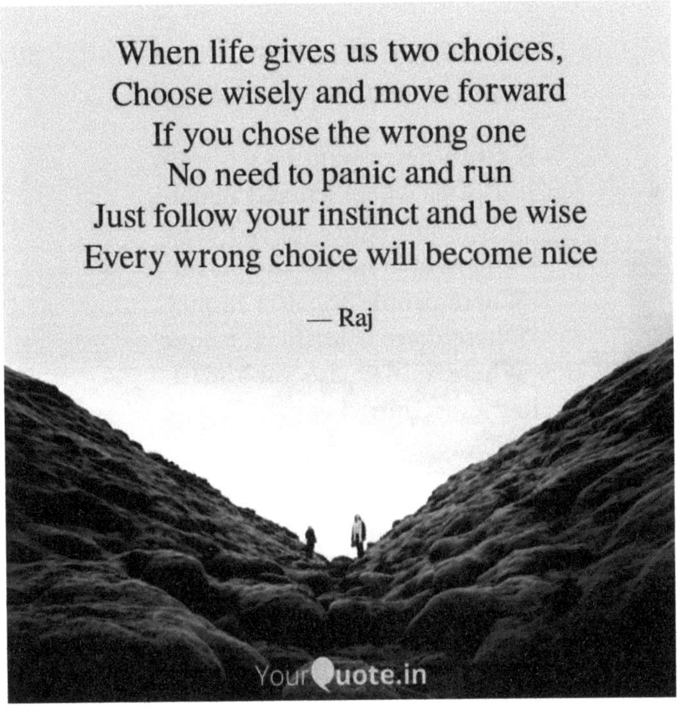
When life gives us two choices,
Choose wisely and move forward
If you chose the wrong one
No need to panic and run
Just follow your instinct and be wise
Every wrong choice will become nice
— Raj
YourQuote.in

Enter Caption

10. A city I never want to see

A City I Never Want To See Again
A city I never want to see again
Is a place where hatered remain
Where humanity doesn't exist
Where love never ever persist
Where people are after money
Where there is artificial honey
Where Smile exists on a mask
Rest everything behind the task
– Raj
YourQuote.in

Enter Caption

11. The stairs to sucess

The stairs to success
Can be climbed any moment
The moment when to climb
To be decided by the person
Once began to climb
Should never look back
Keep going on climbing
Till you get tired and exhausted

— Raj

Enter Caption

12. Nature and calamities

The clouds, wind and the rain
How beautiful is the scene
Followed with thunder and lightning
How enchanting is the rain
Love of the nature towards mankind
Is always magical and enticing
Greenery all over the cosmos
How soothing it feels for the eyes
When humans misuses the natures gift
How painful it is like
Calamities occurs as a sign of protest from the nature
But still the humans don't realise and protect the nature

— Raj

YourQuote.in

Enter Caption

13. The city is tired

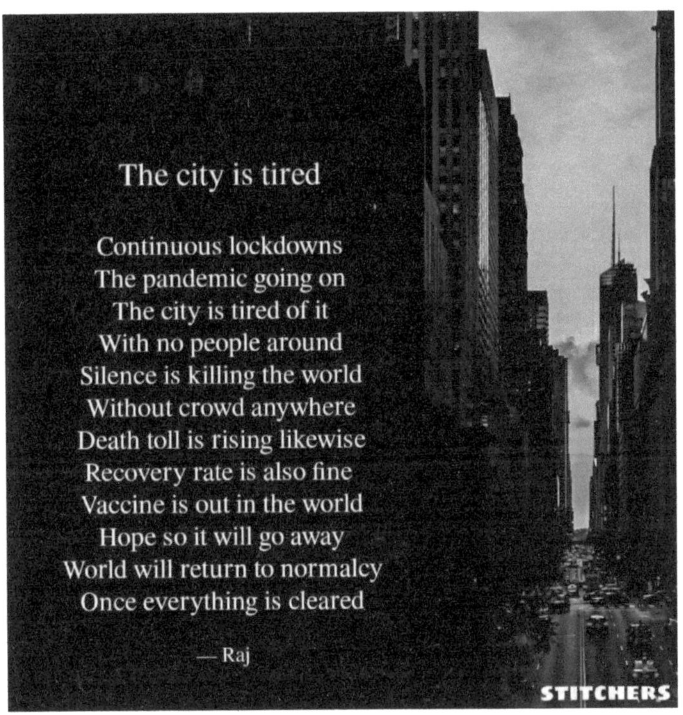
The city is tired
Continuous lockdowns
The pandemic going on
The city is tired of it
With no people around
Silence is killing the world
Without crowd anywhere
Death toll is rising likewise
Recovery rate is also fine
Vaccine is out in the world
Hope so it will go away
World will return to normalcy
Once everything is cleared
— Raj
STITCHERS

Enter Caption

14. Love begins when

LOVE
LOVE
Love begins when
The day you are born
It lasts till the grave
Begning from the mother
Till the day of parting
Everyone loves each other
Once left the world
Still love remains
For days they remember
– Raj

Enter Caption

15. Death

Death

Why are people afraid of it?
It is along with us from the day we are born.
Then why are we afraid of it?
It is the ultimate truth which prevails.
Does any one knows their life span?
The answer is a big no.
Death can knock anyone's door any time
When the span of life completes
the soul has to go back to it's pavilion.
The human body is nothing but a cloth
which the soul wear's.
The soul is a mass of energy.
The body is made up of water, soil, fire and space
And it return back to the soil.
Thus the cycle continues.

– Raj

Enter Caption

16. Depth of the Sea

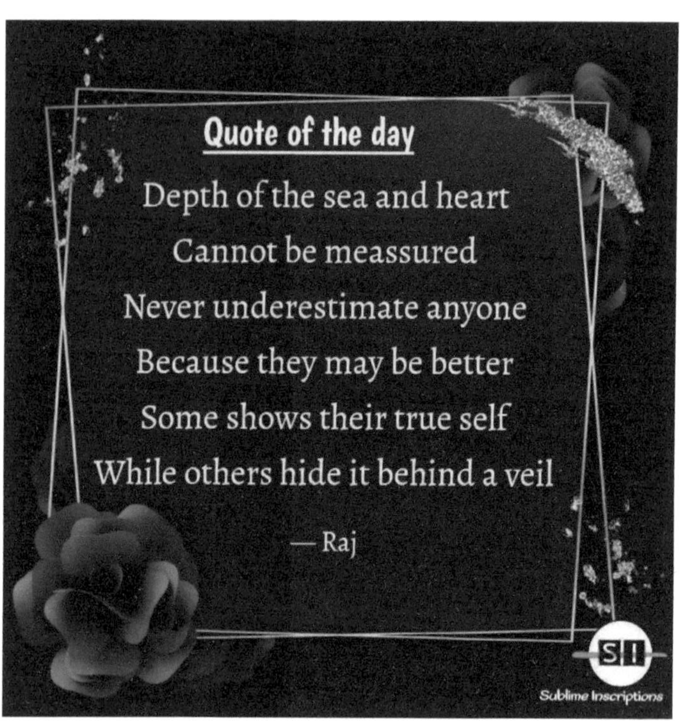
Quote of the day
Depth of the sea and heart
Cannot be meassured
Never underestimate anyone
Because they may be better
Some shows their true self
While others hide it behind a veil
— Raj
SI
Sublime Inscriptions

Enter Caption

17. Destiny decides

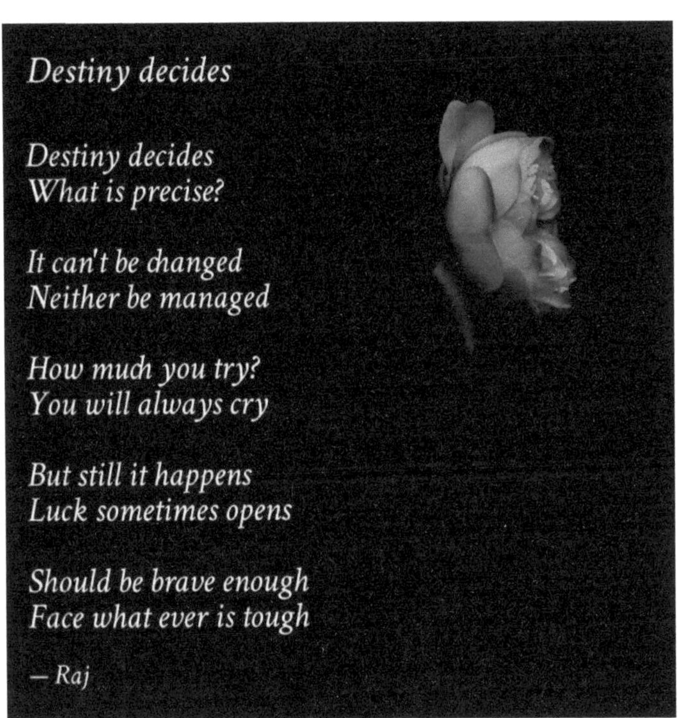
Destiny decides
Destiny decides
What is precise?
It can't be changed
Neither be managed
How much you try?
You will always cry
But still it happens
Luck sometimes opens
Should be brave enough
Face what ever is tough
– Raj

Enter Caption

18. A Diamond is forever

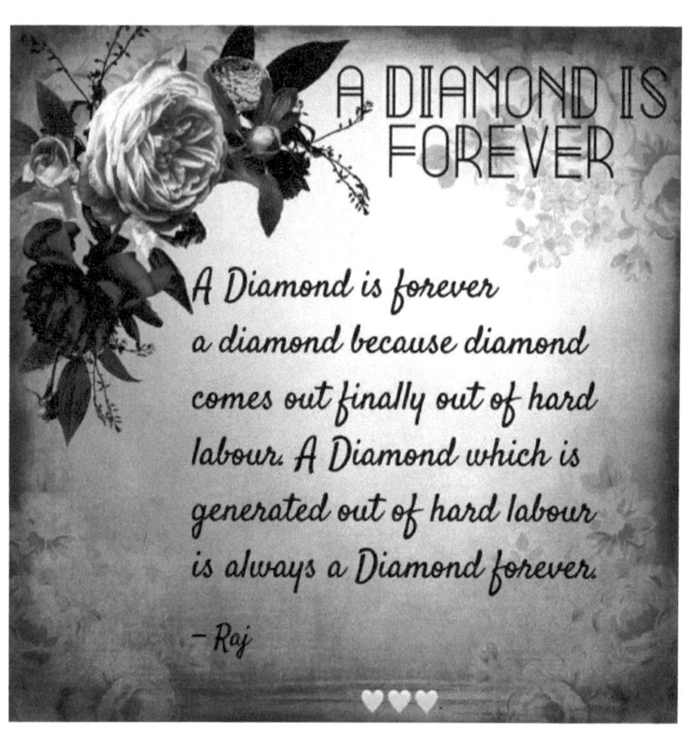
A DIAMOND IS
FOREVER
A Diamond is forever
a diamond because diamond
comes out finally out of hard
labour. A Diamond which is
generated out of hard labour
is always a Diamond forever.
- Raj

Enter Caption

19. Life is a series of

Life is a series of
Different types of games
With a stipulated time limit
Which is to be played well
Failures are too often
Chances of retake is less

— Raj

Enter Caption

20. Dreams are stars

Dreams are stars
Dreams are stars
That twinkle in the sky
Though It can be seen
But can't be reached
Dreams are seen
But some gets fullfilled
Not all those dreams
Seen can get fulfilled
– Raj
YourQuote.in

Enter Caption

21. Without enough sleep

Without enough sleep,
Eyes can't even weep
The whether is so hot
Can not bear the heat

I am on and awake still
And sleep comes until
Till then stare at the sky
Talking to moon and star

Sky is beautiful to look at
Glittering stars in the night
Moon between the stars
Spreading it's love and light

— Raj
YourQuote.in

Enter Caption

22. Fire in my blood

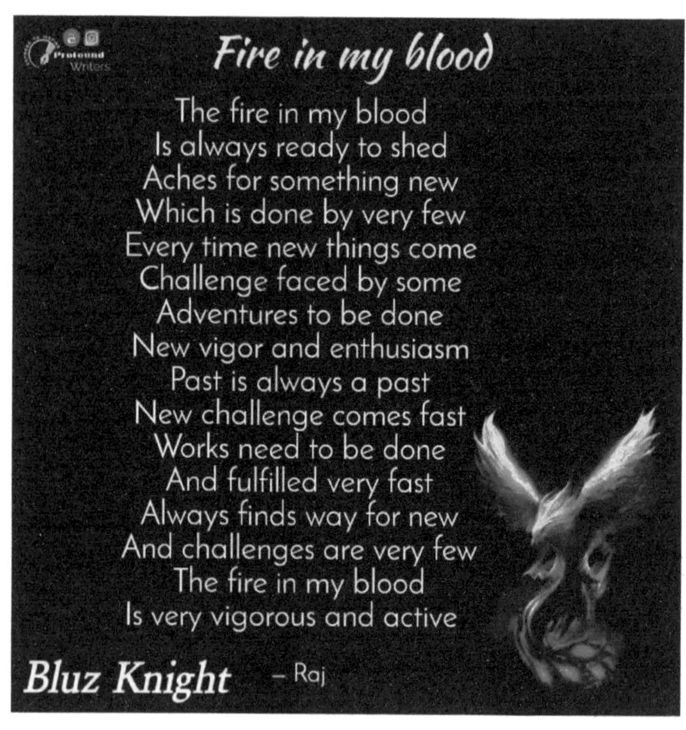
Profound Writers
Fire in my blood
The fire in my blood
Is always ready to shed
Aches for something new
Which is done by very few
Every time new things come
Challenge faced by some
Adventures to be done
New vigor and enthusiasm
Past is always a past
New challenge comes fast
Works need to be done
And fulfilled very fast
Always finds way for new
And challenges are very few
The fire in my blood
Is very vigorous and active
Bluz Knight – Raj

Enter Caption

23. I can't live without

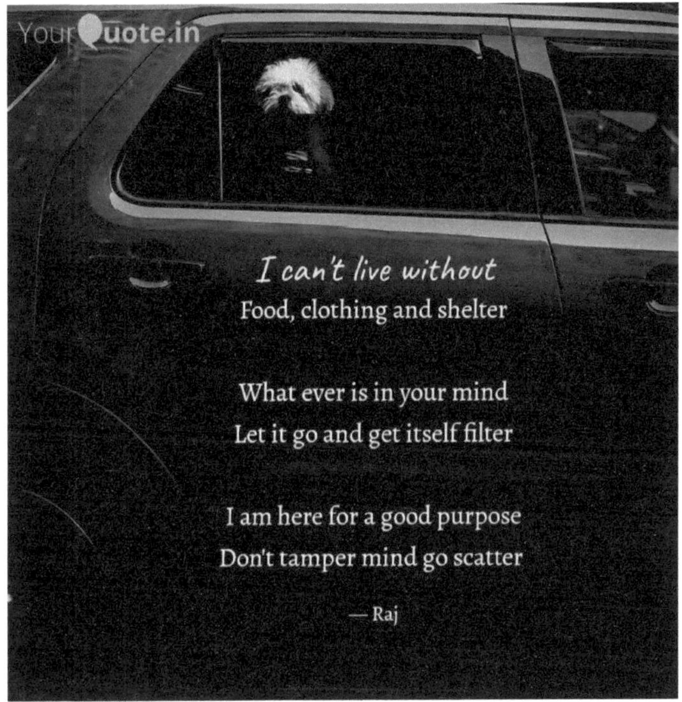
YourQuote.in
I can't live without
Food, clothing and shelter

What ever is in your mind
Let it go and get itself filter

I am here for a good purpose
Don't tamper mind go scatter

— Raj

Enter Caption

24. The window of my room

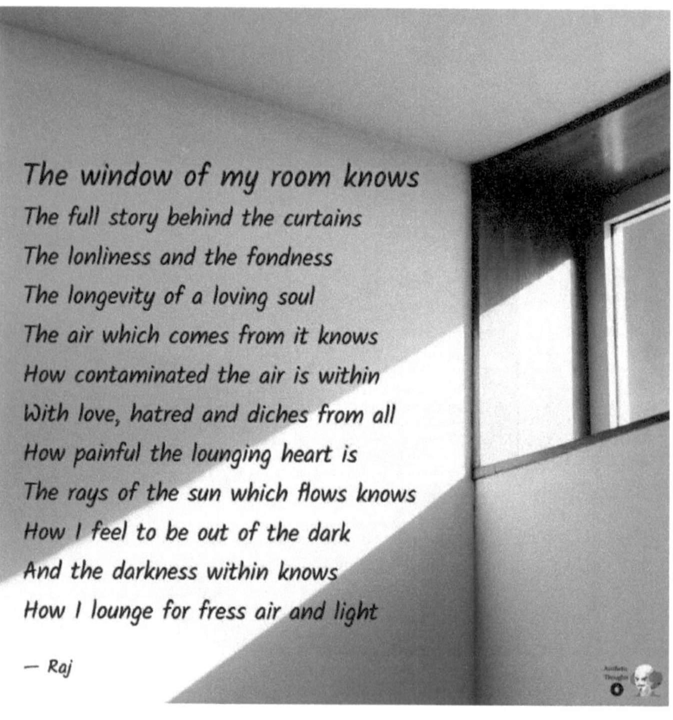
The window of my room knows
The full story behind the curtains
The lonliness and the fondness
The longevity of a loving soul
The air which comes from it knows
How contaminated the air is within
With love, hatred and diches from all
How painful the lounging heart is
The rays of the sun which flows knows
How I feel to be out of the dark
And the darkness within knows
How I lounge for fress air and light
— Raj

Enter Caption

25. The future belongs to

The future belongs to
The future generation's
Giving a doubt about
The present and past generations
Let's forget about the past generations
Which becomes a memory forever
The present generations will never last for long
here and becomes a memory in the future

— Raj

YourQuote.in

Enter Caption

26. Holding back & Letting go

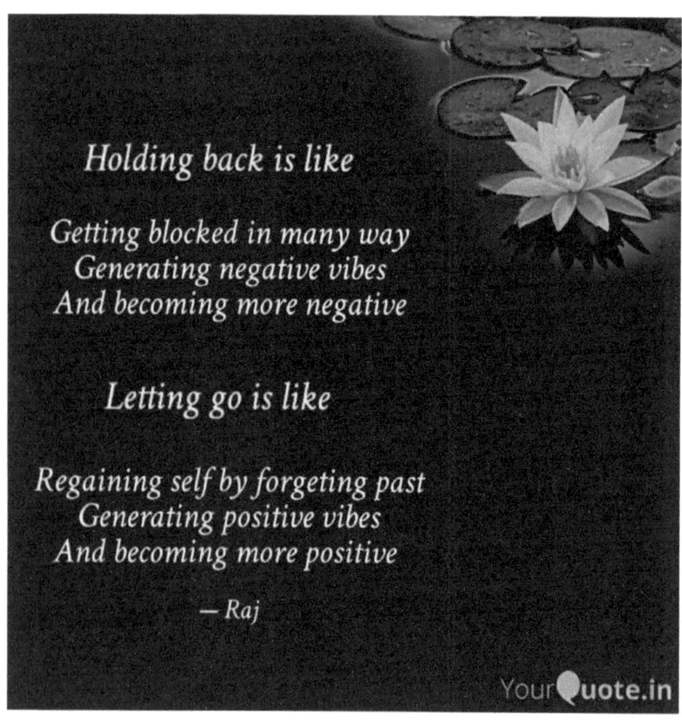
Holding back is like
Getting blocked in many way
Generating negative vibes
And becoming more negative
Letting go is like
Regaining self by forgeting past
Generating positive vibes
And becoming more positive
— Raj
YourQuote.in

Enter Caption

27. Those who hurt other's

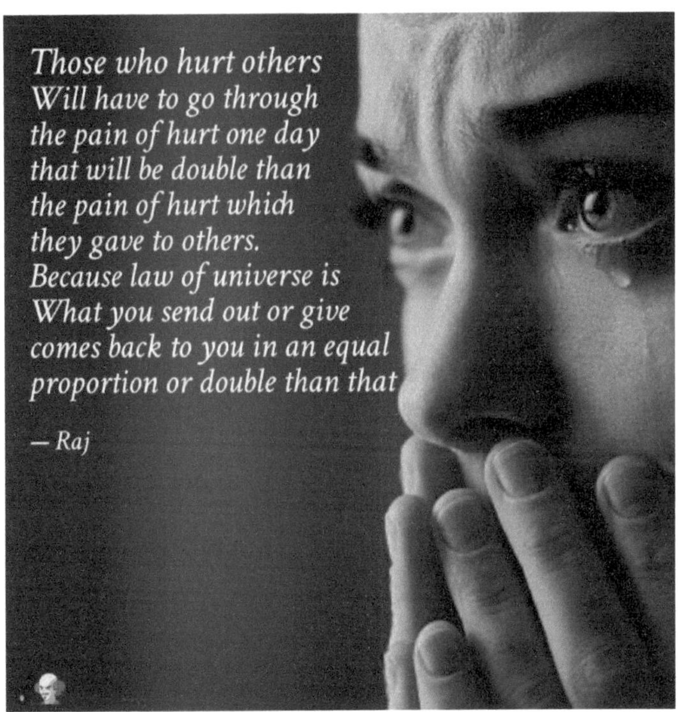
Those who hurt others
Will have to go through
the pain of hurt one day
that will be double than
the pain of hurt which
they gave to others.
Because law of universe is
What you send out or give
comes back to you in an equal
proportion or double than that
— Raj

Enter Caption

28. Hidden love is like

Hidden love is like
Hidden love is like
Killing all the desire
Breath without oxygen
Body without antigen
War without a fight
Moon without light
Tea without sugar
Bread without butter
– Raj

Enter Caption

29. Call yourself beautiful

Call yourself beautiful
However ugly you look
Makes you more beautiful
Thinking of yourself so
Look into the mirror
And say you are beautiful
Beauty doesn't include
The way you always look
It is the beauty of the mind
and a beautiful soul within
Makes you more beautiful
With a pure heart and soul
– Raj

Enter Caption

30. My heart knows

My heart knows
How much it is in need
Love which people speaks
Are very rare to perceive

My heart knows
The pain it went through
To reduce the pain
How it endeavoured

– Raj

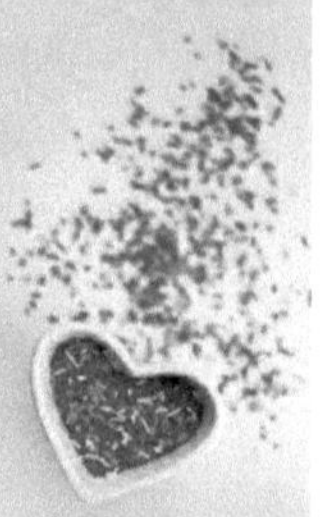

Enter Caption

31. Finally we met

Finally We Met

How to narrate the condition of my heart
which is beyond my comprehension
Wanted to meet my beautiful who
lost her heart to me and myself to her
God forbidened my intention by
bringing the epidemic
Commuting stopped completely by
lockdown of all people
Roads were deserted and neither
could people come out of their homes
There were many hurdles as we were
stuck up at two different places
Meeting was not possible except by
social media networks and video calls
There began a hope of meeting when
slowly lockdown was getting lifted
Finally we met when lockdowns got lifted

– Raj

•Profound Writers Gleam•

Enter Caption

32. I became love addicted

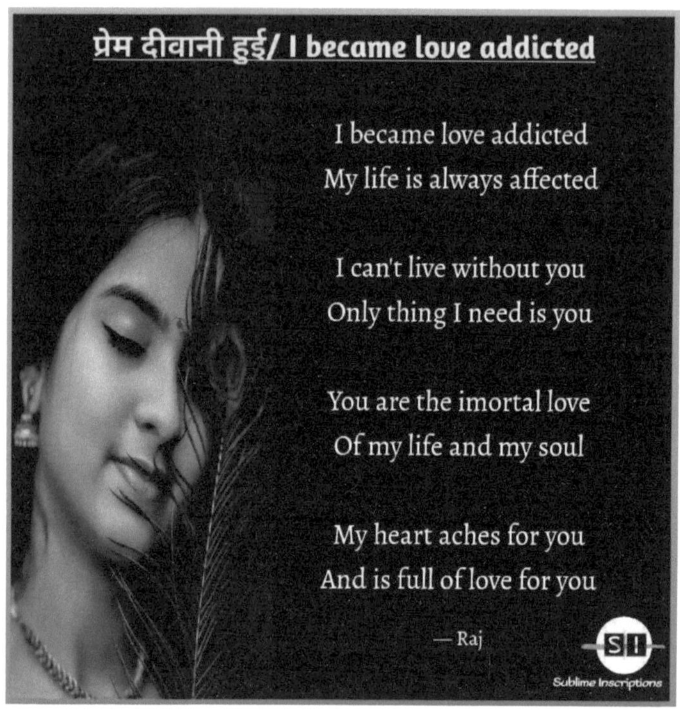
प्रेम दीवानी हुई/ I became love addicted
I became love addicted
My life is always affected
I can't live without you
Only thing I need is you
You are the imortal love
Of my life and my soul
My heart aches for you
And is full of love for you
— Raj
SI
Sublime Inscriptions

Enter Caption

33. Morning once said to night

Morning once said to the night
I come every time and bring light
Drakness erodes the peoples mind
Where I spread everytime the light

The night said to the morning in reply
I come and relax everybody's minds
By giving them time to sleep at night
Charging them fully to take the plight

— Raj

YourQuote.in

Enter Caption

34. If I were a falling leaf

If I were a falling leaf,

If I were a falling leaf
I would fall away right
Paving the way for new
And leaving a message

Every young leaf here
Would become old one day
And fall off from the group
Disconnecting one self

Never laugh on a falling leaf
One day will come for you
To fall off from the group
And go to the other world

— Raj

YourQuote.in

Enter Caption

35. I was living in darkness

I was living in darkness

I was living in darkness
In my eyes always wetness
Life was a bit angry with me
Out of blue the light appears

Love is a part where it hurts
Lonliness starts to dwell in heart
Heart says past is past forget it
Subconscious keeps reminding it

— Raj

Enter Caption

36. I Love U

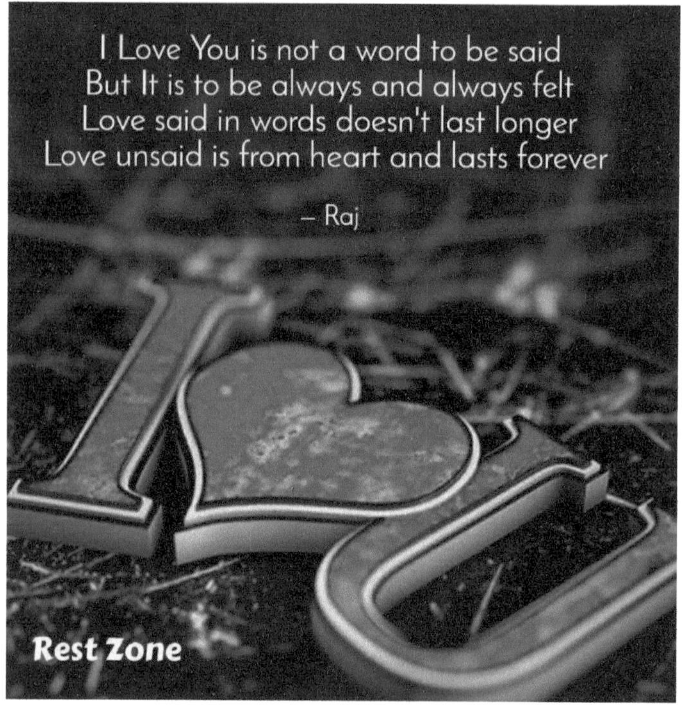
I Love You is not a word to be said
But It is to be always and always felt
Love said in words doesn't last longer
Love unsaid is from heart and lasts forever
– Raj
Rest Zone

Enter Caption

37. Deceit to Myself

Profound Writers
Deceit to myself
I still believed in her
Being known the truth
I kept loving her so much
Knowing she is not mine
Knew It was deciet to myself
Where she was an addiction
Couldn't be able to forget
Keep heart in my control
Kept all time deceiving myself
Couldn't control my mindset
Wish to come out of this
And be honest with myself
– Raj
••APOGEE••

Enter Caption

38. Decisions

DECISIONS
It is very difficult to take decision
Once on the edge if a cross road
If the decision taken is correct
You will be on the correct path
If it is wrong every thing will go wrong
So right decision taken at right time
Is always correct and be on right path
Follow the intuition and make decision
Decision's is an important aspect of Life
Thus take right decision and proceed
– Raj
•• APOGEE ••

Enter Caption

39. If the sun could talk

If the sun could talk,
It would say how it is hot

Feeling of the warmth it spreads
Making the people always dread

The pain which is the cause
To shed the fire without a pause

How the plants and humans effect
Without it's precense there is no life

– Raj

YourQuote.in

Enter Caption

40. I wish I could

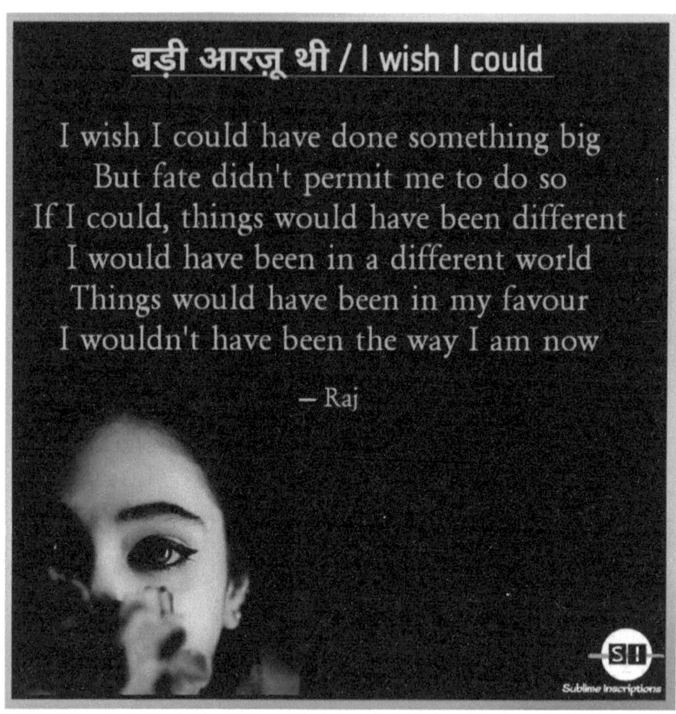

बड़ी आरज़ू थी / I wish I could
I wish I could have done something big
But fate didn't permit me to do so
If I could, things would have been different
I would have been in a different world
Things would have been in my favour
I wouldn't have been the way I am now
– Raj
SI
Sublime Inscriptions

Enter Caption

41. There is a special thing

There's a special thing
about my past
Which keeps revolving
around me fast
The more I try to forget it
The more it engulfs me tight
At last it ends in a mind fight
Alas again it begins with fright
— Raj

Enter Caption

42. Life goes on

Life goes on

Life goes on and on
For what ever the reson
It doesn't stop for any one
Just keeps moving forward
Untill the day you reach
Your destined destination

– Raj

♥♥♥.

Enter Caption

43. Life teaches

Life teaches

Life teaches us many life lessons
Which is not taught in academics
Experiences makes people perfect
Still it keeps on teaching something
In life every day is a new chapter
Book of life completes when life ends

– Raj

Enter Caption

44. Loneliness makes us realize

Loneliness makes us realize
Lonliness makes us realize
How beautiful is the life
When there is no crowd
Alone and feeling proud
There is no tension and stress
And have no one to impress
Just concentrate on ones self
With tranquility everywhere
- Raj

Enter Caption

45. Loneliness teaches people

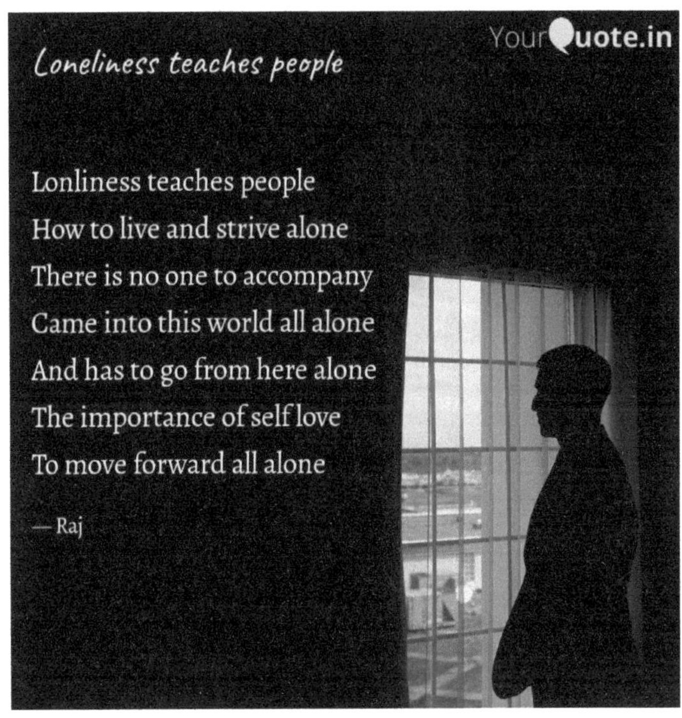
YourQuote.in
Loneliness teaches people
Lonliness teaches people
How to live and strive alone
There is no one to accompany
Came into this world all alone
And has to go from here alone
The importance of self love
To move forward all alone
— Raj

Enter Caption

46. The city breathes

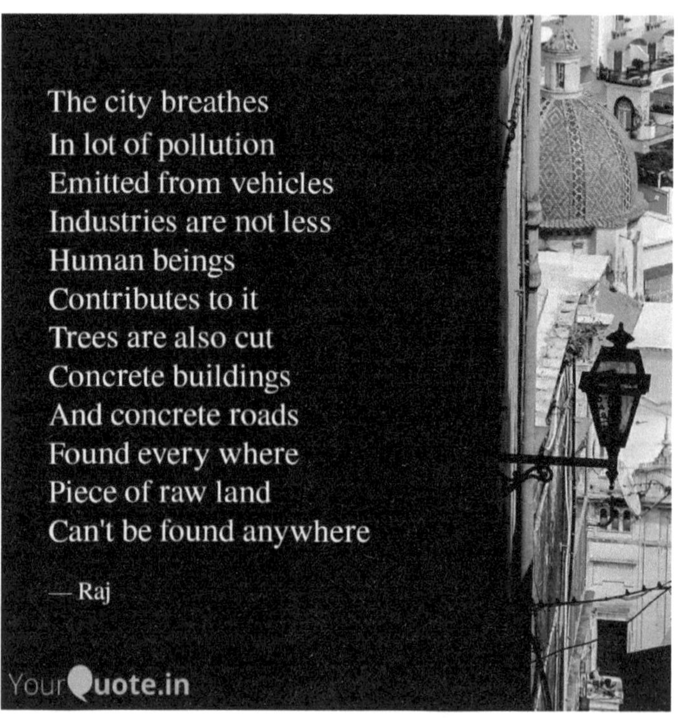

The city breathes
In lot of pollution
Emitted from vehicles
Industries are not less
Human beings
Contributes to it
Trees are also cut
Concrete buildings
And concrete roads
Found every where
Piece of raw land
Can't be found anywhere
— Raj
YourQuote.in

Enter Caption

47. Love is that bookmark

Love is that bookmark

Love is that bookmark
Which can be read again
The never ending pain
And the hidden happiness
If you miss a book of love
Another will follow suit
It is a never ending story
Which goes throughout life

— Raj

YourQuote.in

Enter Caption

48. If love didn't exist

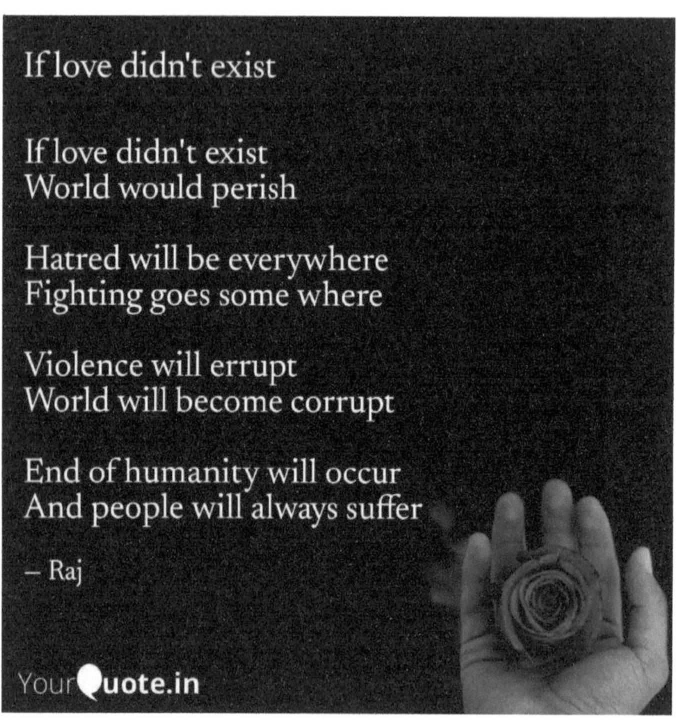
If love didn't exist
If love didn't exist
World would perish
Hatred will be everywhere
Fighting goes some where
Violence will errupt
World will become corrupt
End of humanity will occur
And people will always suffer
– Raj
YourQuote.in

Enter Caption

49. Love left me when

Love left me when

Love left me when I was in dire need of her
Left me to the fate to deal with it whatever

Loneliness is only thing which I retrieved
And it is much better than and relieved

I have learned that Love is a sweet poison
It is better to keep away from its unison

— Raj

YourQuote.in

Enter Caption

50. Meditation

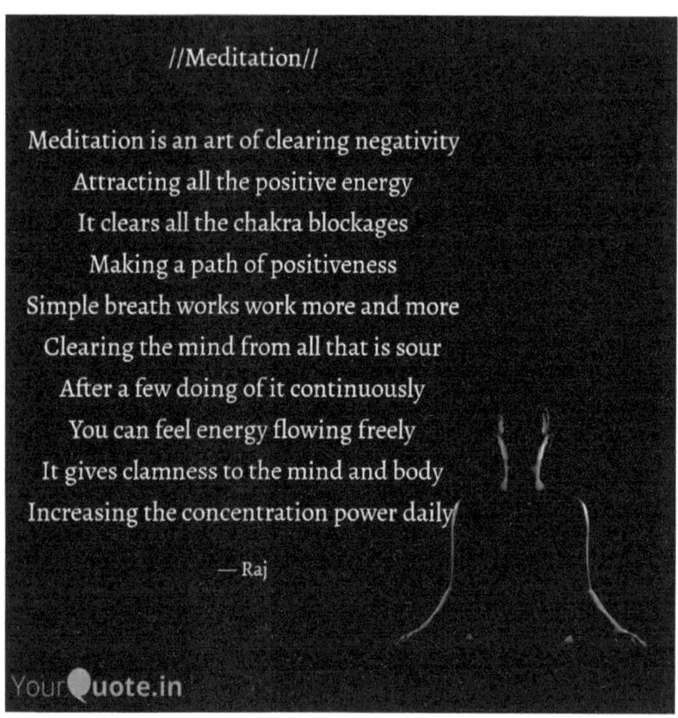
//Meditation//
Meditation is an art of clearing negativity
Attracting all the positive energy
It clears all the chakra blockages
Making a path of positiveness
Simple breath works work more and more
Clearing the mind from all that is sour
After a few doing of it continuously
You can feel energy flowing freely
It gives clamness to the mind and body
Increasing the concentration power daily
— Raj
YourQuote.in

Enter Caption

51. The moment I sit

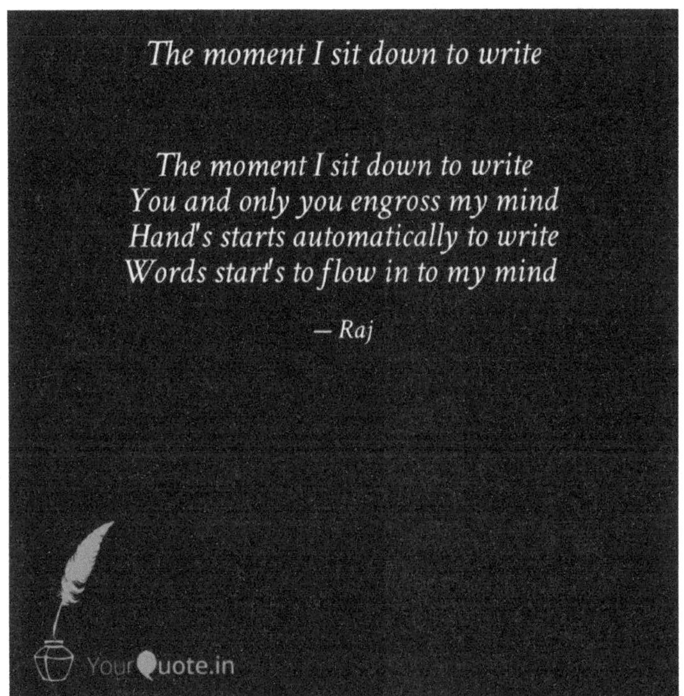
The moment I sit down to write
The moment I sit down to write
You and only you engross my mind
Hand's starts automatically to write
Words start's to flow in to my mind
— Raj
YourQuote.in

Enter Caption

52. Every night, I expect

Every night, I expect
The moon to aspect

The sky and the stars
Along with the lunars

You and me holding hands
Watching it laying on sands

— Raj

Enter Caption

53. Blank Paper

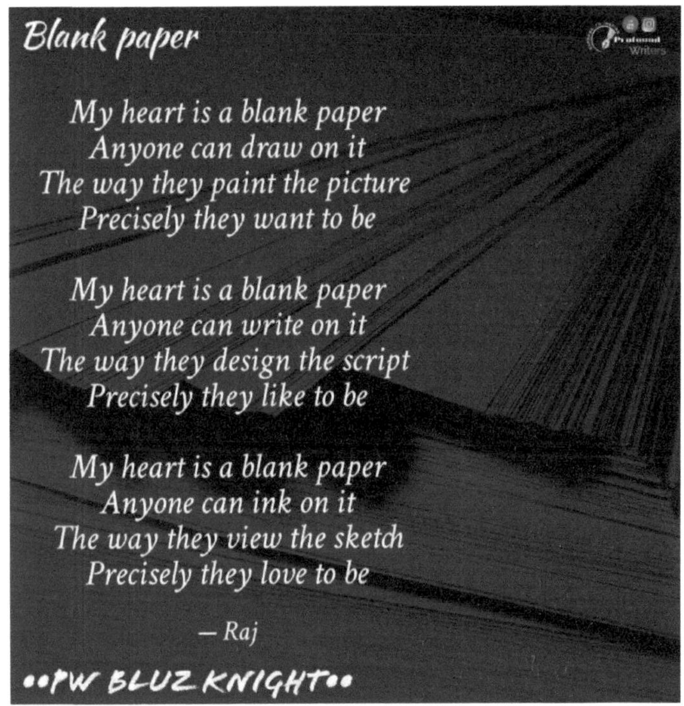
Blank paper
Profound Writers
My heart is a blank paper
Anyone can draw on it
The way they paint the picture
Precisely they want to be
My heart is a blank paper
Anyone can write on it
The way they design the script
Precisely they like to be
My heart is a blank paper
Anyone can ink on it
The way they view the sketch
Precisely they love to be
— Raj
••PW BLUZ KNIGHT••

Enter Caption

54. My mission in life

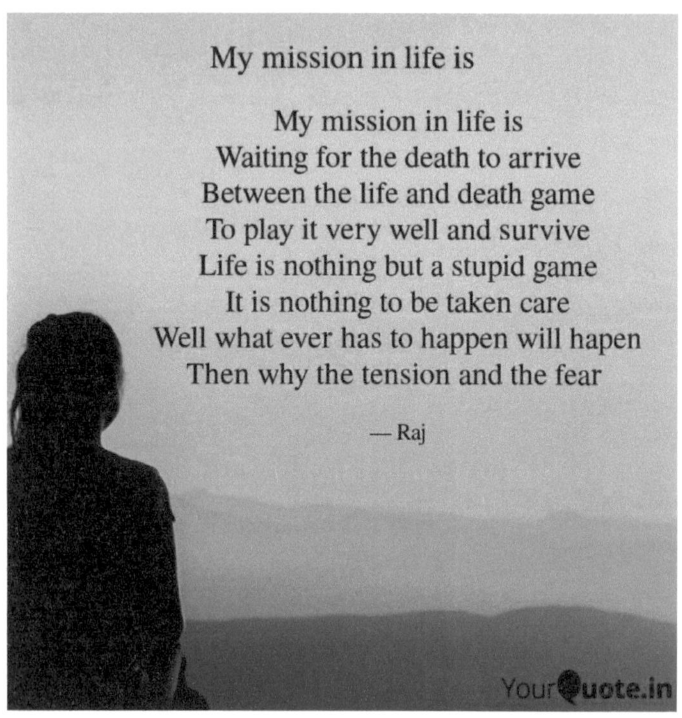
My mission in life is
My mission in life is
Waiting for the death to arrive
Between the life and death game
To play it very well and survive
Life is nothing but a stupid game
It is nothing to be taken care
Well what ever has to happen will hapen
Then why the tension and the fear
— Raj
YourQuote.in

Enter Caption

55. Nature

//Nature//
The beautiful face of yours
Feels like seeing more of you
It aches my heart so much
To see you and only you
Beauty of you makes me crazy
To admire the beauty of you
Take each and every snap of you
Fulfilling my hearts desire of you
— Raj
YourQuote.in

Enter Caption

56. Never ending feelings

//Never ending Feelings//
When I look at the sky
I feel like flying
When I look into the ocean
I feel like diving
When I look at the universe
I feel like exploring
When I look in to your eyes
I feel like loving
— Raj
YourQuote.in

Enter Caption

57. Night is a window

Night is a window
Night is a window
Which has to endow
Waiting for new day
Which is on its way
To be explored with
Positive vibes that stays
— Raj
Democrats & Dissenters

Enter Caption

58. A night without dreams

A night without dreams is like
A night without dreams is like
Having a tea without sugar
A night without star's is like
A blank paper without words
A night without you is like
A chocolate without sweetness
— Raj
YourQuote.in

Enter Caption

59. Only silence can convey

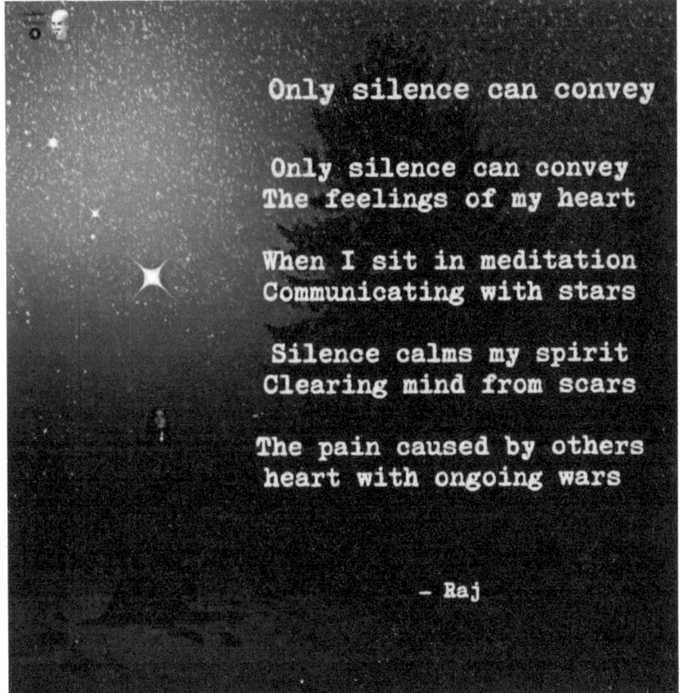
Only silence can convey
Only silence can convey
The feelings of my heart
When I sit in meditation
Communicating with stars
Silence calms my spirit
Clearing mind from scars
The pain caused by others
heart with ongoing wars
- Raj

Enter Caption

60. Be like books

Be like books
Pages filled with
Full of knowledges
Spread knowledge
To the readers
Love them for ever
Without expecting
— Raj

Enter Caption

61. Broken heart

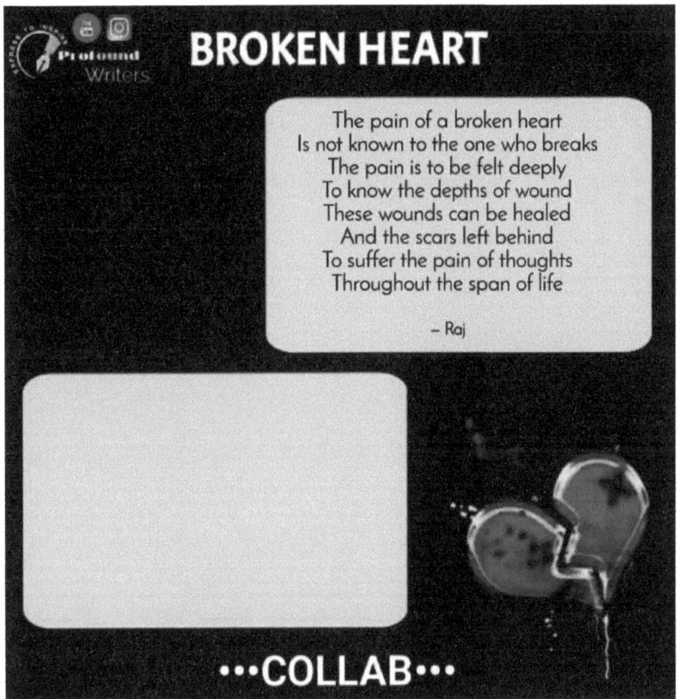
Profound
Writers
BROKEN HEART
The pain of a broken heart
Is not known to the one who breaks
The pain is to be felt deeply
To know the depths of wound
These wounds can be healed
And the scars left behind
To suffer the pain of thoughts
Throughout the span of life
– Raj
•••COLLAB•••

Enter Caption

62. The beauty we see

The beauty we see
Is a part of illusion
The beauty we feel
Is a part of intuition

The beauty of heart
Is a perfect imagination
The beauty of soul
Is a perfect combination

– Raj

Enter Caption

63. Live for today

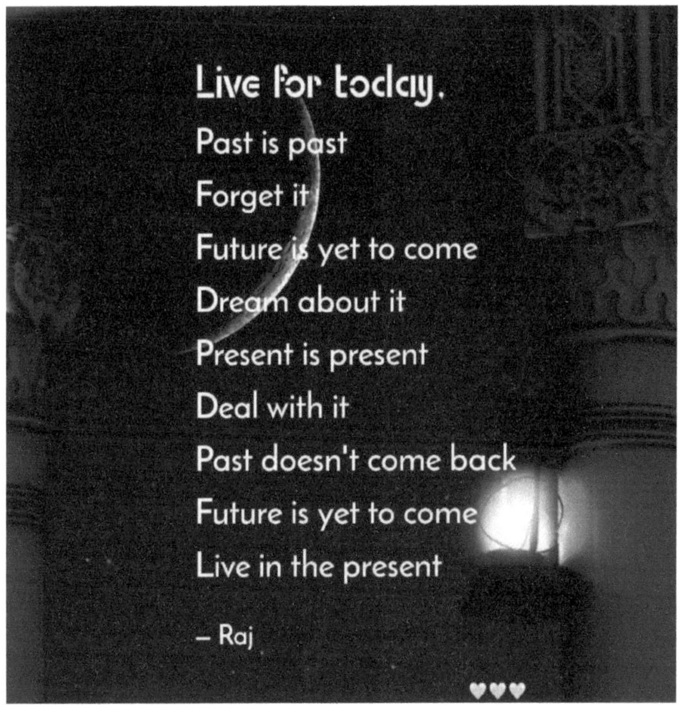
Live for today.
Past is past
Forget it
Future is yet to come
Dream about it
Present is present
Deal with it
Past doesn't come back
Future is yet to come
Live in the present
– Raj

Enter Caption

64. Peace is

Peace is
Peace is something
Which is not available
Not in this prevailing world
Don't know about other world
Searched every where
But couldn't find it any where
Except with you in my arms
Available when you are around
— Raj

Enter Caption

65. You left and I'm fine

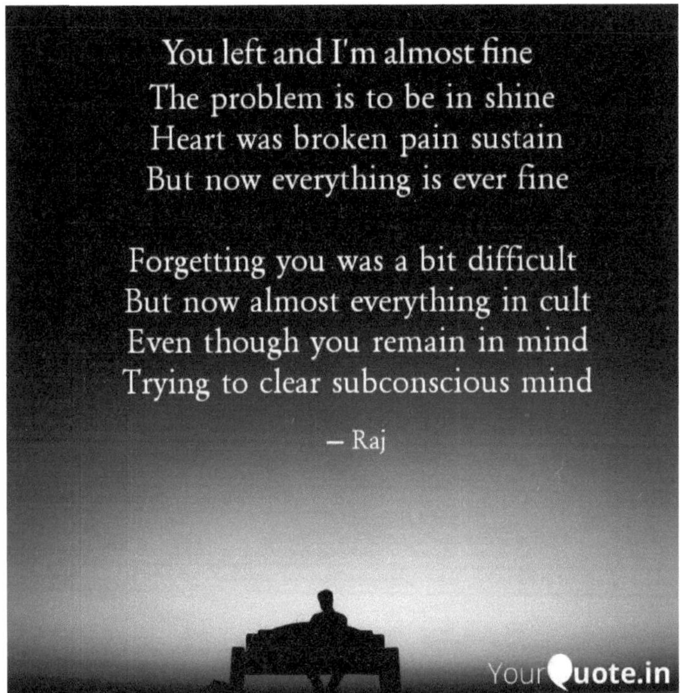
You left and I'm almost fine
The problem is to be in shine
Heart was broken pain sustain
But now everything is ever fine

Forgetting you was a bit difficult
But now almost everything in cult
Even though you remain in mind
Trying to clear subconscious mind

– Raj

YourQuote.in

Enter Caption

66. Purification of body

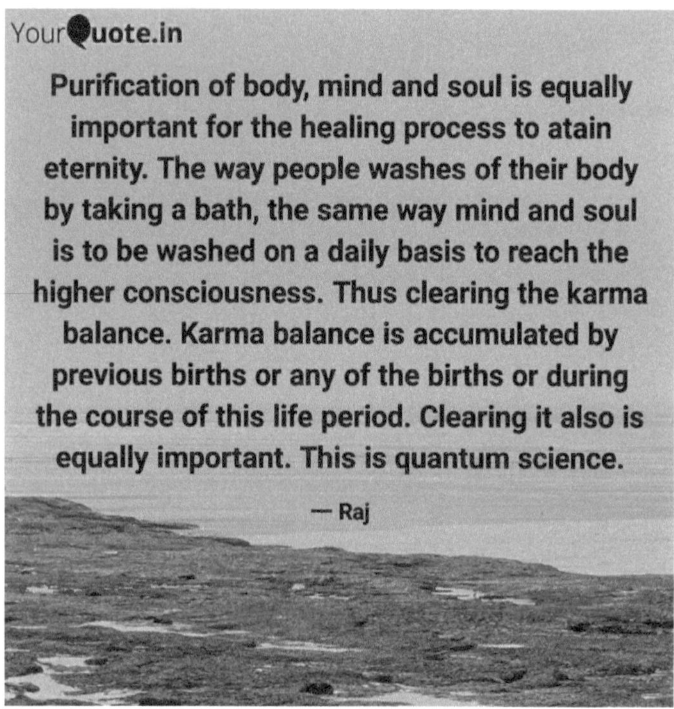
YourQuote.in
Purification of body, mind and soul is equally important for the healing process to atain eternity. The way people washes of their body by taking a bath, the same way mind and soul is to be washed on a daily basis to reach the higher consciousness. Thus clearing the karma balance. Karma balance is accumulated by previous births or any of the births or during the course of this life period. Clearing it also is equally important. This is quantum science.
— Raj

Enter Caption

67. To attain something

//Quotes of the Day//
To attain something in life
You will always need to strive
There is no thing like magic in Life
Unless you work hard and strive
— Raj

Enter Caption

68. Let go off the passerby's

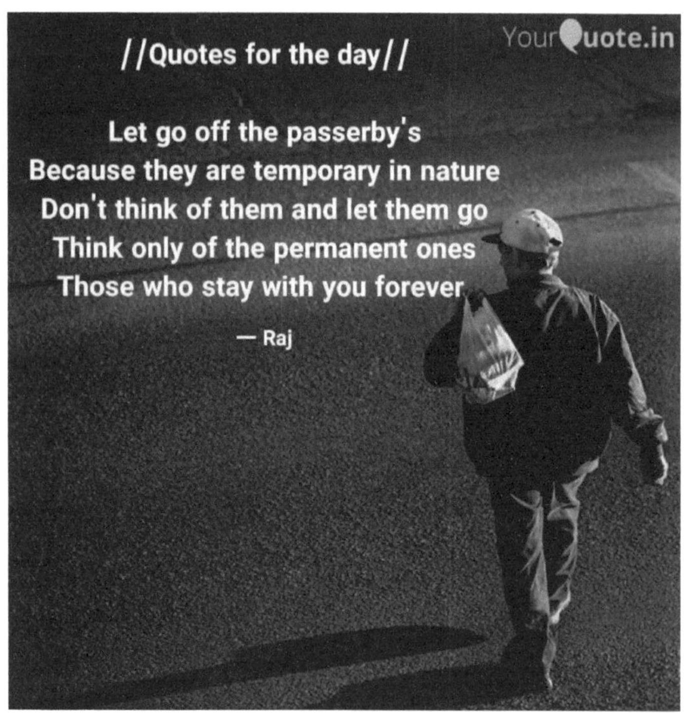
YourQuote.in
//Quotes for the day//
Let go off the passerby's
Because they are temporary in nature
Don't think of them and let them go
Think only of the permanent ones
Those who stay with you forever
— Raj

Enter Caption

69. Life teaches us

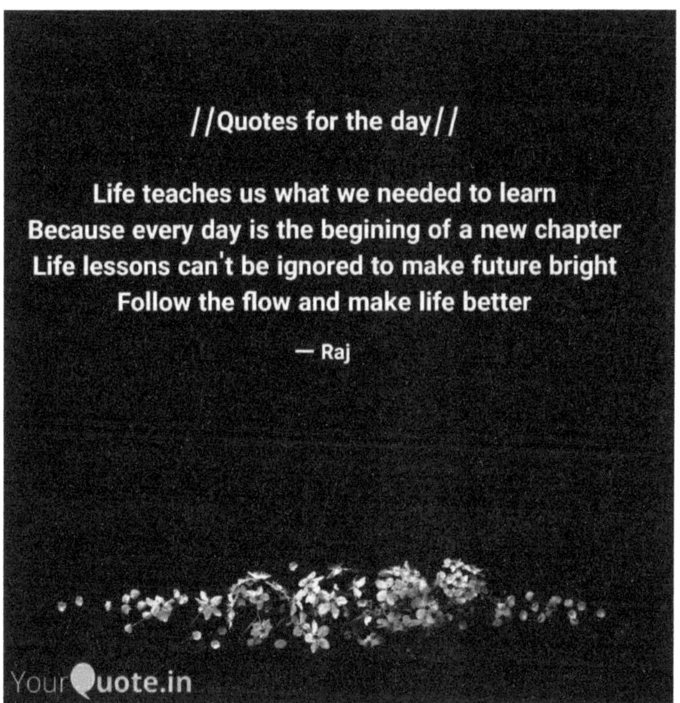
//Quotes for the day//
Life teaches us what we needed to learn
Because every day is the begining of a new chapter
Life lessons can't be ignored to make future bright
Follow the flow and make life better
— Raj
YourQuote.in

Enter Caption

70. A witch says money

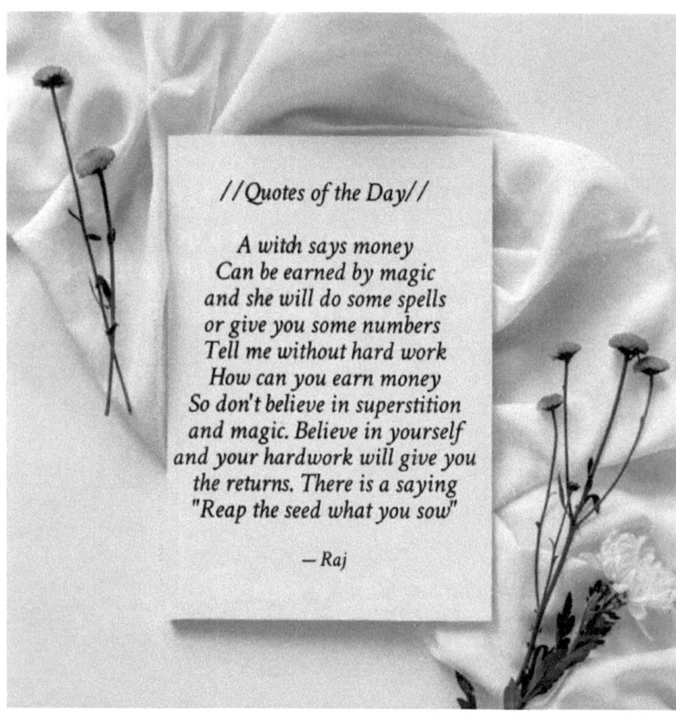
//Quotes of the Day//

A witch says money
Can be earned by magic
and she will do some spells
or give you some numbers
Tell me without hard work
How can you earn money
So don't believe in superstition
and magic. Believe in yourself
and your hardwork will give you
the returns. There is a saying
"Reap the seed what you sow"

– Raj

Enter Caption

71. Nobody can heal

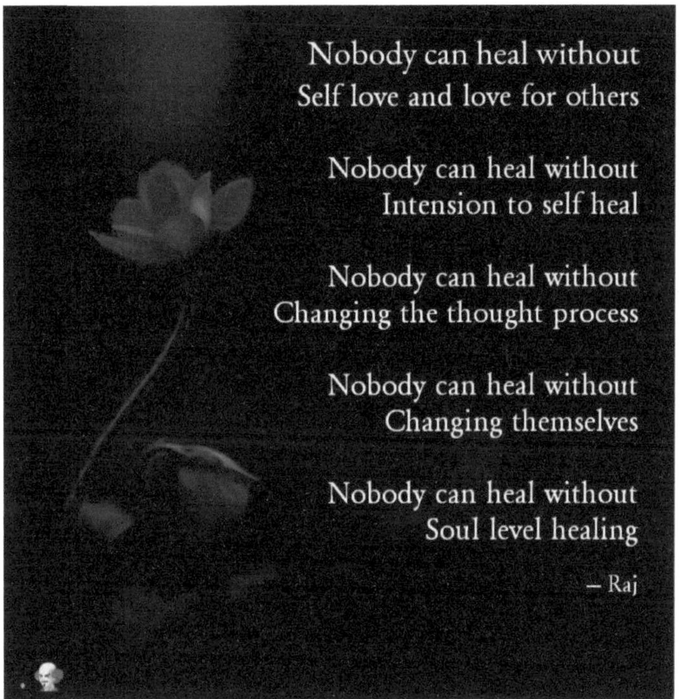
Nobody can heal without
Self love and love for others
Nobody can heal without
Intension to self heal
Nobody can heal without
Changing the thought process
Nobody can heal without
Changing themselves
Nobody can heal without
Soul level healing
– Raj

Enter Caption

72. The shadow of my past

The shadow of my past
The shadow of my past
Keeps hunting me vast
How much I try to forget
It makes me much regret
Past is not which I want
New begning is the best
Let the life take a new turn
Begin it with confidence and run
— Raj
YourQuote.in

Enter Caption

73. The distance between us

The distance between us
Is similar to sky and earth

Let's curtail the distance
And get too closer at once

Once you are somewhat near
Let's make our love for ever

— Raj

Rest Zone

Enter Caption

74. We are living in a world

We're living in a world where
The soil is coloured in bloodshed
And the atmosphere with hatered
Voilence erupted everywhere
Killings happening every now and there
Safety of women and children is a concern
Real men's are not seen anywhere
People running helter-skelter for life
Crying and screaming to get help
Terrorists are seen everywhere
Trying to get powerful than the rest
Killing innocent lives and spreading terror everywhere

— Raj

CASCADE WRITERS

Enter Caption

75. Expectations are like

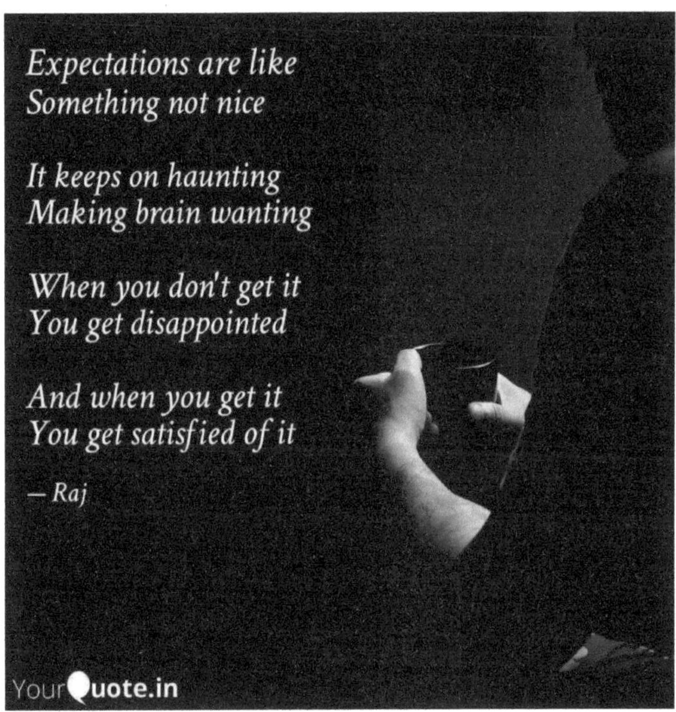
Expectations are like
Something not nice

It keeps on haunting
Making brain wanting

When you don't get it
You get disappointed

And when you get it
You get satisfied of it

— Raj
YourQuote.in

Enter Caption

76. If stars lose their shine

If stars lose their shine

If stars lose their shine
Darkness will fill the night
Cosmos will be very Scarry
Humans will lose energy
Galaxy will be very dark
Dark powers will raise heads
Question of survival will arise
Humans and other living beings
Will not be able to sustain

– Raj

Democrats & Dissenters

Enter Caption

77. When we learn to sacrifice

When we learn to sacrifice
We start sacrificing everything
For one reason or the other
It becomes fashion type of thing
Heart gets used to the hurt's
Sacrificing love type of thing
People start's to play with us
Like we are always a play thing
Hurting more and more our sentiments
Like our heart is like stone type of thing

— Raj

Enter Caption

78. A wise man once

A wise man once forgot to say
That there is a million dream
Which remains unfulfilled
And needs to be fulfilled
Without hard word no dreams comes true
There is no magic unless you come through
— Raj
YourQuote.in

Enter Caption

79. When the end is near

When the end is near
There is no need to fear
Every movie has begining
And an end very near
Life is high definition movie
Which is always very dear
But has to end one day
So why there is a fear
– Raj

Enter Caption

80. Those who love darkness

Those who love darkness
Those who love darkness
Will never love brightness
They are always thoughtful
And also every time hopeful
Optmistic are there nature
And can reach any stature
Life seems nothing to them
And learn to deal with them
Darkness shows us the devil
Which is hidden behind the veil
It makes us learn how to deal
All that is hidden and said evil
— Raj

Enter Caption

81. If you love someone

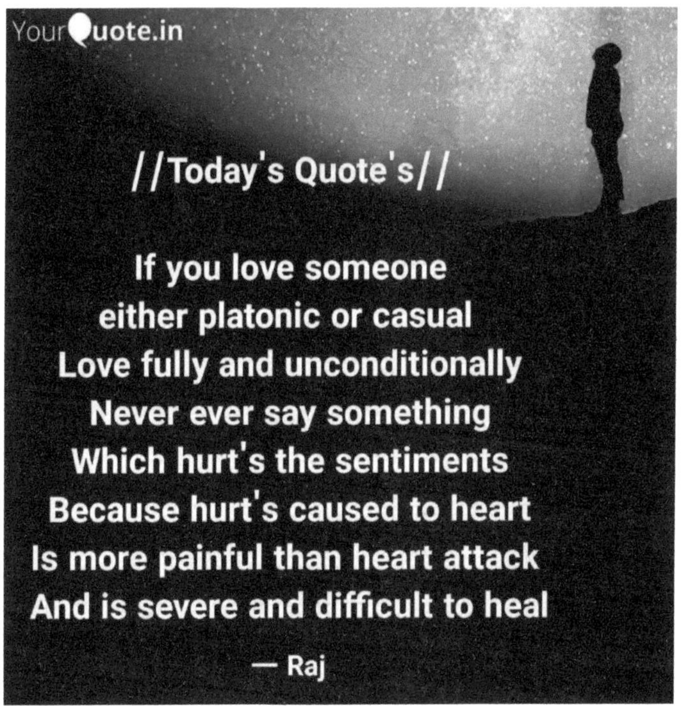
YourQuote.in
//Today's Quote's//
If you love someone
either platonic or casual
Love fully and unconditionally
Never ever say something
Which hurt's the sentiments
Because hurt's caused to heart
Is more painful than heart attack
And is severe and difficult to heal
— Raj

Enter Caption

82. The wored needs more

The world needs more
Tolerance and tranquility
Without which worlds
balance goes off
Intermittent war begins
Tranquility is compromised
Poluting the environment
With poisonous gas
Cost of human lives etc..
Are effects of after war
— Raj
YourQuote.in

Enter Caption

83. Although life is unpredictable

Although life is unpredictable,
We can't stop living here
Let's move with the hope
Everything will be fine
Life has it's due course
It completes by itself
Let's take it as a game
And make it more fun like
—Raj

Enter Caption

84. Keep your heart open

Keep your heart open for
Unconditional Love
Unlimited happiness
Life long Friendship
All time relatives
Not for
Unconditional Hatred
Unlimited Sadness
Lifetime Envy's
All time Enemies
— Raj
OPEN

Enter Caption

85. Under the tree of Love

Under the tree of love,
Under the tree of love
Everyone is infected
Love is that type of virus
That needs to be circulated
In every drop of blood
Whidh flows in the veins
Untill it redhes the four
Chambers of the heart
So that it spreads to all
Hearts in the universe
— Raj

Enter Caption

86. Source of Life

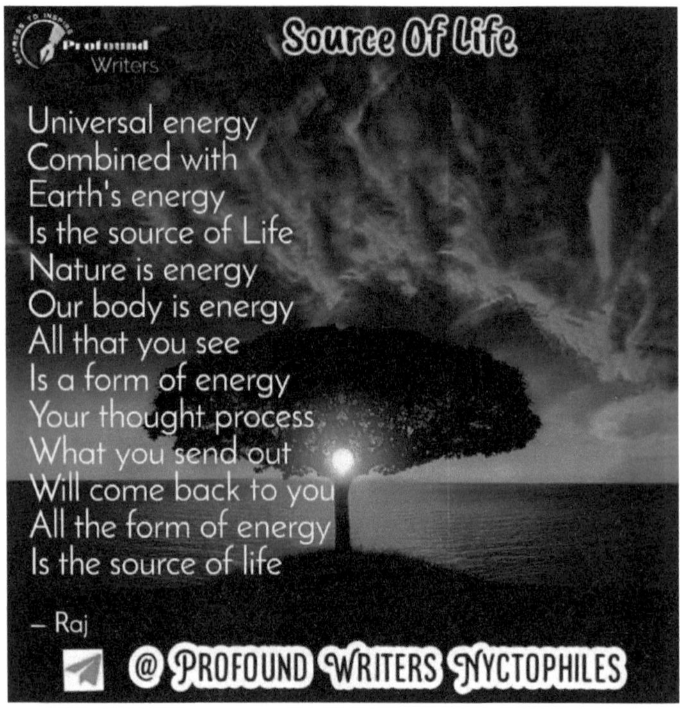
Express to Inspire
Profound
Writers
Source Of Life
Universal energy
Combined with
Earth's energy
Is the source of Life
Nature is energy
Our body is energy
All that you see
Is a form of energy
Your thought process
What you send out
Will come back to you
All the form of energy
Is the source of life
– Raj
@ Profound Writers Nyctophiles

Enter Caption

87. Burn those thoughts

Burn those thoughts
That unknown thoughts
Gives you much trouble
Burn those thoughts
that doesn't serves you
Negative thought pattern
Leaves you in negativity
Burn those negativity
And be always positive
– Raj

Enter Caption

88. Up's and downs

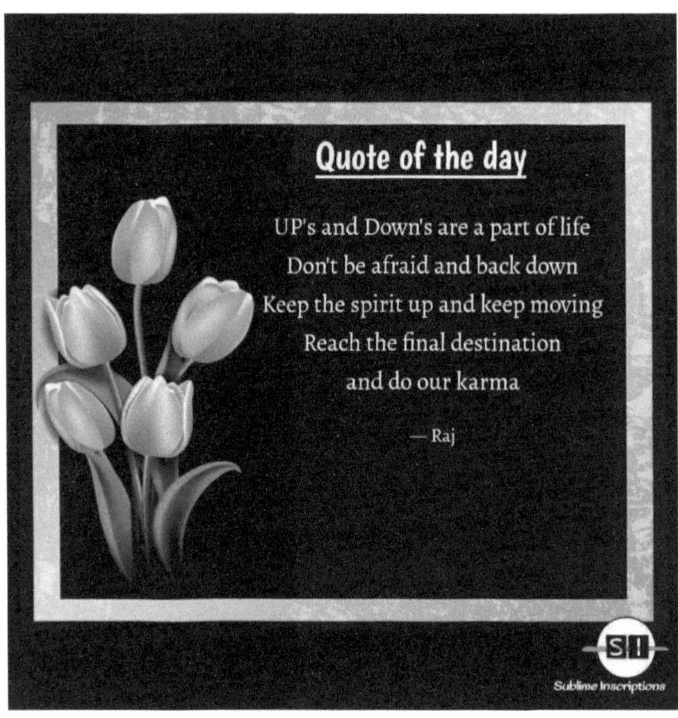

Quote of the day
UP's and Down's are a part of life
Don't be afraid and back down
Keep the spirit up and keep moving
Reach the final destination
and do our karma
— Raj
SI
Sublime Inscriptions

Enter Caption

89. The symptoms of love

The symptoms of love
Is very difficult to understand
And the one who understood
Never observed and accepted
Night long spend without sleep
Day long with mind wandering
If asked them what's the matter
Would say effect of sleepless night
– Raj

Enter Caption

90. Walking alone

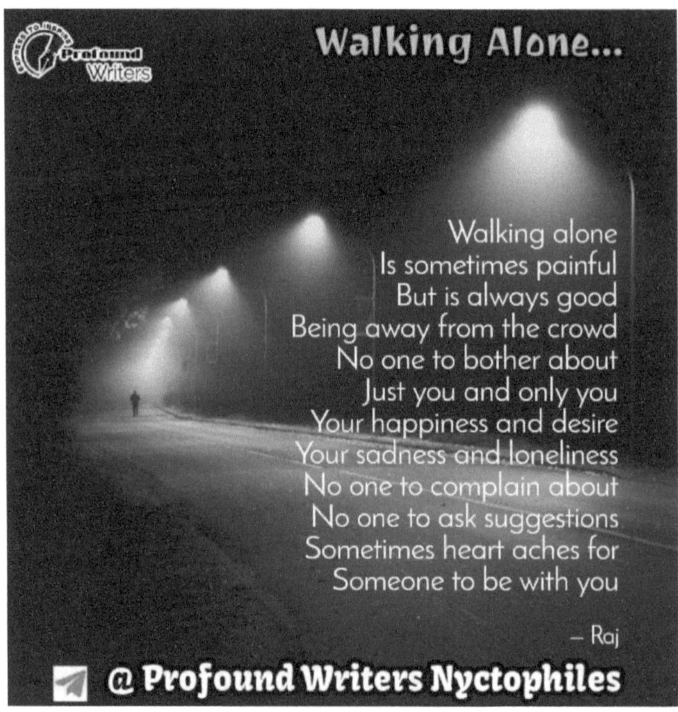
Profound Writers
Walking Alone...
Walking alone
Is sometimes painful
But is always good
Being away from the crowd
No one to bother about
Just you and only you
Your happiness and desire
Your sadness and loneliness
No one to complain about
No one to ask suggestions
Sometimes heart aches for
Someone to be with you
– Raj
@ Profound Writers Nyctophiles

Enter Caption

91. When I lost you

When I lost you, I lost
When I lost you, I lost my soul
I am only a body without a soul
Just moving around and around
Lost somewhere in between crowd
Feels like there is nothing in life
Lonliness takes over without a wife
- Raj

Enter Caption

92. When the Queen of Darkness

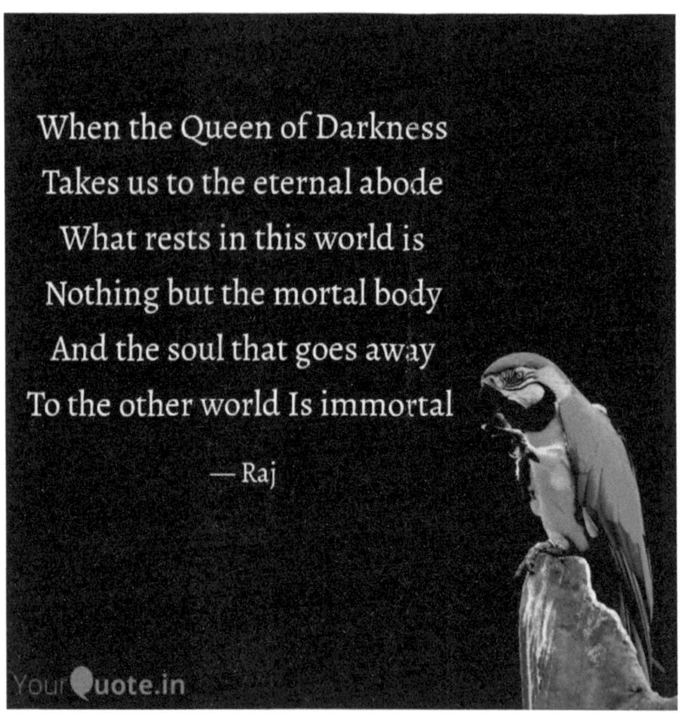
When the Queen of Darkness
Takes us to the eternal abode
What rests in this world is
Nothing but the mortal body
And the soul that goes away
To the other world Is immortal
— Raj
YourQuote.in

Enter Caption

93. When you lose hope

Rest Zone
When you lose hope
When you lose hope
And find there is no scope
Never be afraid and flow
Go along with it in a glow
Be courageous enough
So that hope remains tough
– Raj

Enter Caption

94. A true guru is one

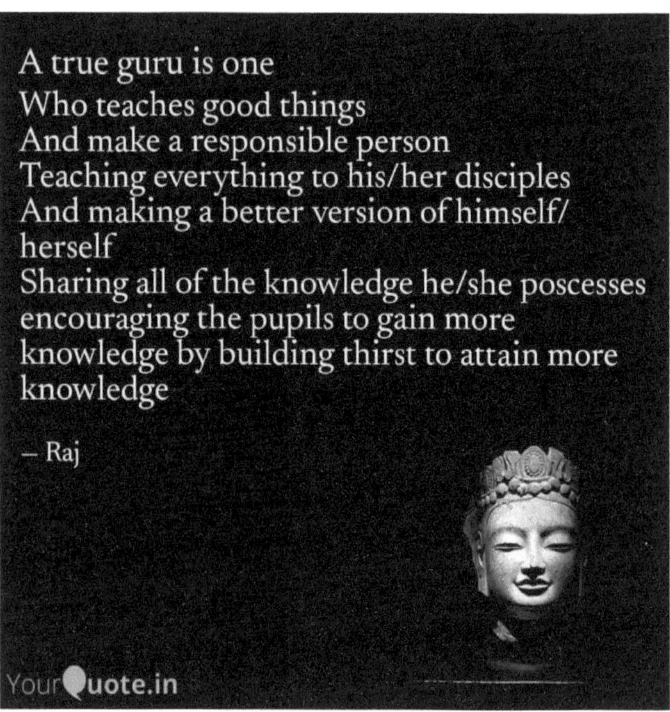
A true guru is one
Who teaches good things
And make a responsible person
Teaching everything to his/her disciples
And making a better version of himself/
herself
Sharing all of the knowledge he/she poscesses
encouraging the pupils to gain more
knowledge by building thirst to attain more
knowledge
– Raj
YourQuote.in

Enter Caption

95. I'm always alone

I'm always alone
Wish to be with
But still I'm alone
No one with me

I love loneliness
Cause I was alone
Since a long time
Became introvert

Wish to socialise
Can't be in crowd
Now I'm afraid
If there is a crowd

– Raj

Enter Caption

96. Women of 21st century

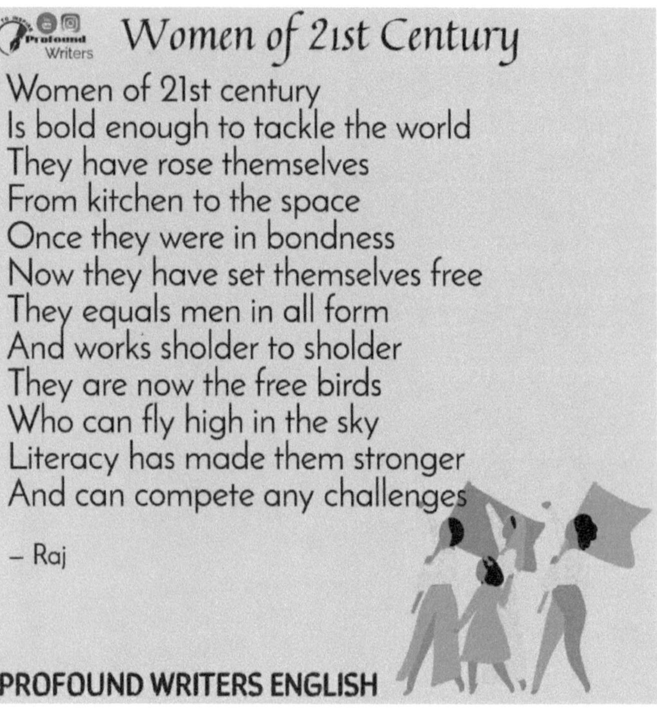
Profound
Writers
Women of 21st Century
Women of 21st century
Is bold enough to tackle the world
They have rose themselves
From kitchen to the space
Once they were in bondness
Now they have set themselves free
They equals men in all form
And works sholder to sholder
They are now the free birds
Who can fly high in the sky
Literacy has made them stronger
And can compete any challenges
– Raj
PROFOUND WRITERS ENGLISH

Enter Caption

97. Yin and yang

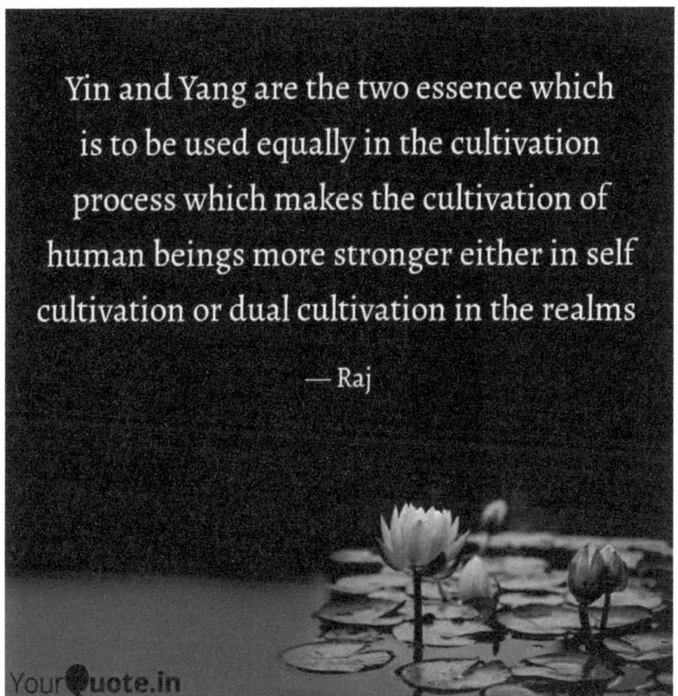
Yin and Yang are the two essence which
is to be used equally in the cultivation
process which makes the cultivation of
human beings more stronger either in self
cultivation or dual cultivation in the realms
— Raj
YourQuote.in

Enter Caption

98. It wasn't my mistake

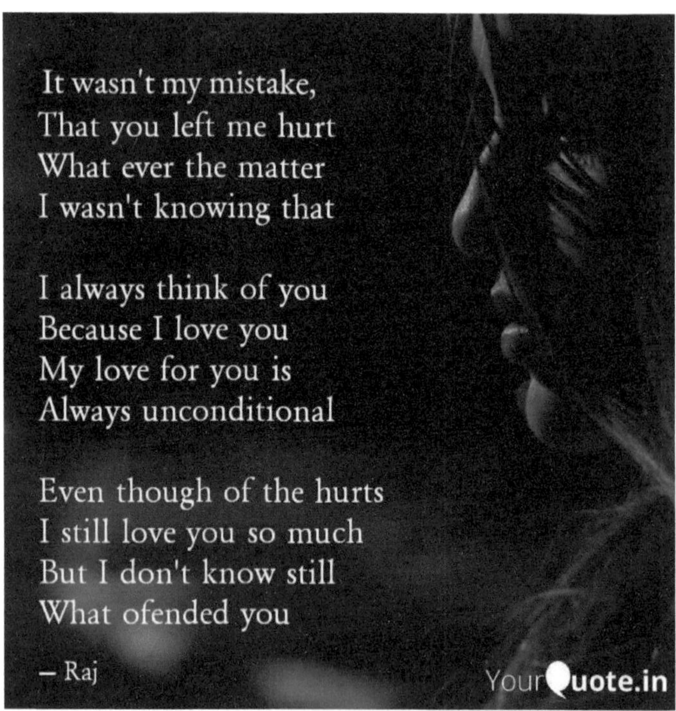
It wasn't my mistake,
That you left me hurt
What ever the matter
I wasn't knowing that

I always think of you
Because I love you
My love for you is
Always unconditional

Even though of the hurts
I still love you so much
But I don't know still
What ofended you

– Raj
YourQuote.in

Enter Caption

99. Dear Death

Rest Zone
Dear Death,
You are the only true friend
From birth along side of life
You are always with me everywhere
Till my right time to depart comes
You are the truth and only friend
Whom I can rely with in my life
You are the shadow of my life
You are welcomed with full heart
– Raj

Enter Caption

100. Your mesmerising eyes

Your mesmerising eyes
The beauty and its shine

Your luscious and red lips
The sweetness of the smile

Your silky and shining hair
And every beautiful strands

Is such a beautiful scene
To be seen and admired

— Raj

Enter Caption

Disclaimer

All creations are based on fiction. It has nothing to do with the life of the author or anyone in the universe. All articles are fictitious and bear no resemblance to any person living or dead. If there is any similarity, it is just coincidence.

Author's Bio

The author belongs to a middle-class family. From childhood, he used to make quick poetry, say and forget it. A close friend of his once noticed this and forced him to write whatever Poems or Quotes he wrote and since then he started writing. He kept his poetry and Quotes to himself and his close friends until he found a platform to write his works online. He is an active writer on the Your Quote site and has received numerous testimonials and certifications for the contest. He is a multilingual writer and his writing is awe-inspiring. Be it English, Hindi, Urdu, Malayalam and Marathi, he excels in all languages. He is also a great inspiration to many intriguing writers. He is a graduate from Mumbai University. He is an accountant and also a self-educated computer engineer. His skills are top notch and he holds several certifications. His passions are acting, writing, painting and dance and listening to music etc…etc….

For feedback:

Mail: shreeraj_m@yahoo.co.uk

9 798887 496573

Printed by Libri Plureos GmbH in Hamburg, Germany